T0025014

What's in this book

This book belongs to

_____

1 Learn about Pinyin 拼音知多少

Pinyin 拼音

1 What is Pinyin? Do you know? Learn about it.

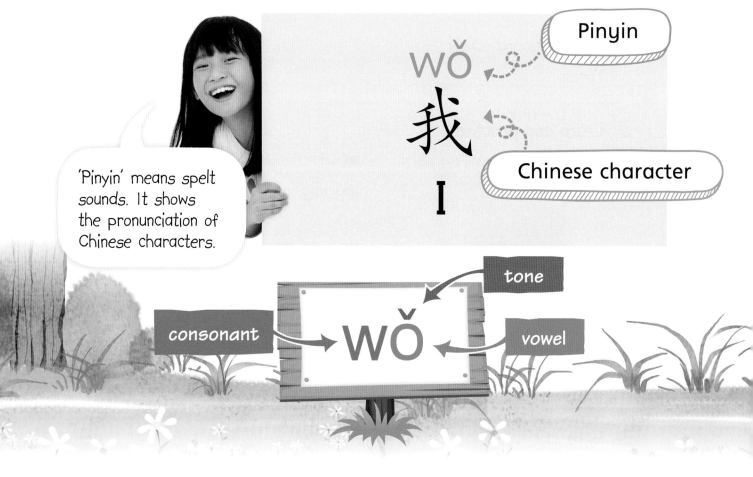

'Pinyin' means spelt sounds. It shows the pronunciation of Chinese characters.

wǒ — Pinyin

我 — Chinese character

I

consonant → Wǒ ← vowel

tone

2 Colour the apples with Pinyin red.

十   cat   nǐ   hē   old

tā   jump   天   不

Consonants and vowels 声母和韵母

1 Look and listen.

Consonants (23)								
b	p	m	f	d	t	n	l	
g	k	h	j	q	x			
zh	ch	sh	r	z	c	s		
y	w							

Vowels (24)									
a	o	e	i	u	ü				
ai	ei	ui	ao	ou	iu	ie	üe	er	
an	en	in	un	ün					
ang	eng	ing	ong						

2 Colour the fish with consonants purple and the ones with vowels green.

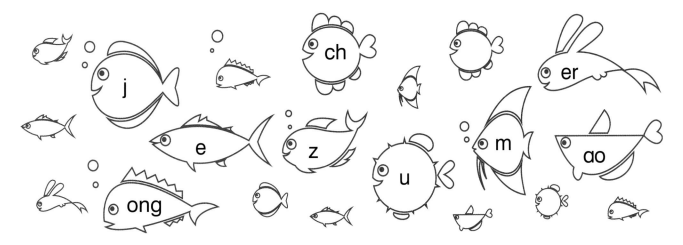

Tones 声调

02 **1** Learn the tones of Pinyin.

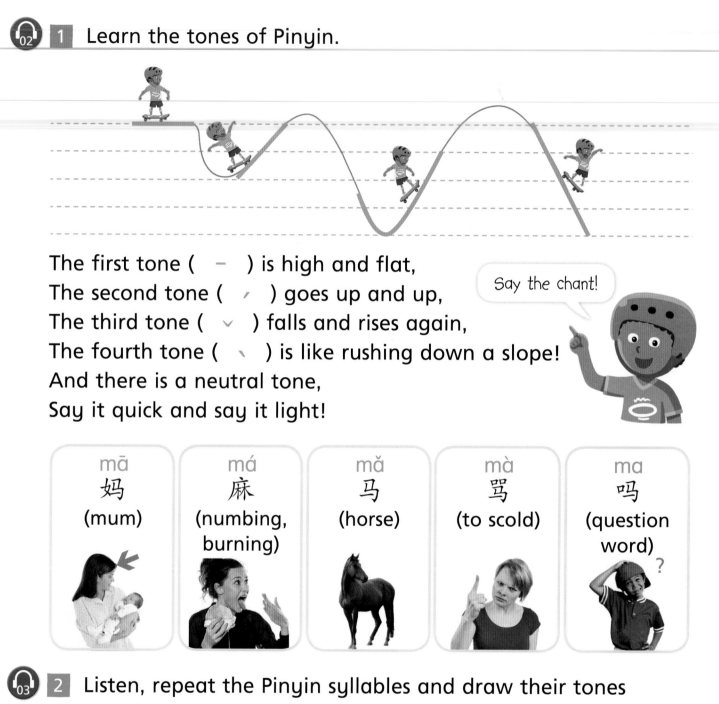

The first tone (ˉ) is high and flat,
The second tone (ˊ) goes up and up,
The third tone (ˇ) falls and rises again,
The fourth tone (ˋ) is like rushing down a slope!
And there is a neutral tone,
Say it quick and say it light!

Say the chant!

mā	má	mǎ	mà	ma
妈	麻	马	骂	吗
(mum)	(numbing, burning)	(horse)	(to scold)	(question word)

03 **2** Listen, repeat the Pinyin syllables and draw their tones with your finger.

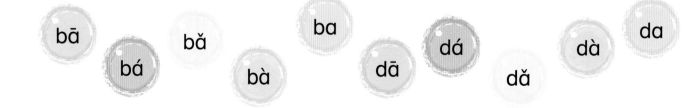

bā bá bǎ bà ba dā dá dǎ dà da

4

2 Learn and practise 学学练练

Single vowels 单韵母

04 1 Learn the single vowels and read them in the different tones.

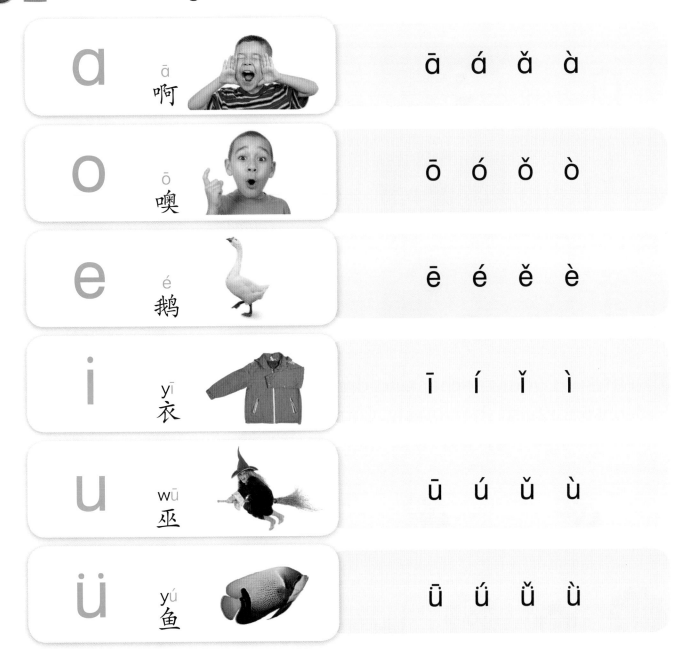

a ā 啊		ā á ǎ à
o ō 噢		ō ó ǒ ò
e é 鹅		ē é ě è
i yī 衣		ī í ǐ ì
u wū 巫		ū ú ǔ ù
ü yú 鱼		ū ú ǔ ù

2 Listen to your teacher and point to the single vowels above.

Consonants 声母 (1)

 1 Learn the consonants and spell the Pinyin syllables on the building blocks.

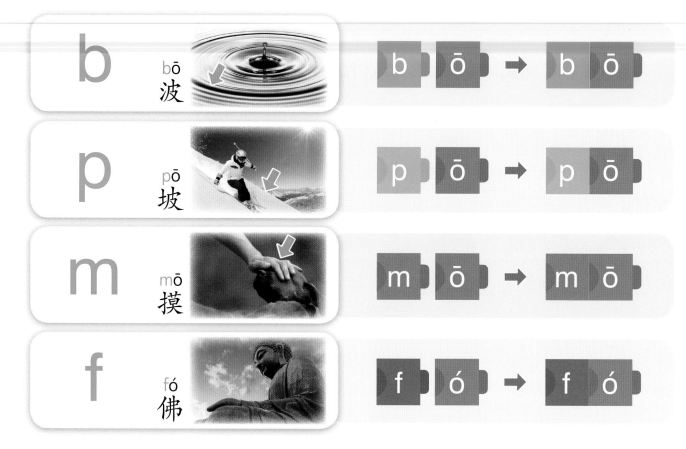

b	bō 波	b ō → b ō
p	pō 坡	p ō → p ō
m	mō 摸	m ō → m ō
f	fó 佛	f ó → f ó

2 Listen to your teacher and draw lines to match the consonants to the vowels. Combine them to form Pinyin syllables and read them aloud.

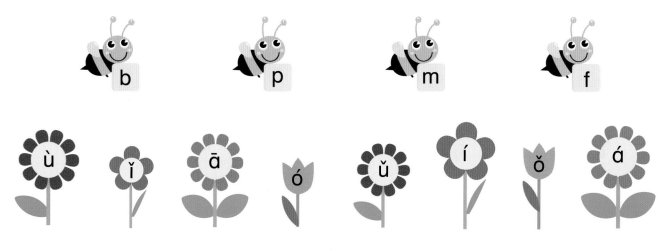

b   p   m   f

ù   ǐ   ā   ó   ǔ   í   ǒ   á

Consonants 声母 (2)

1 Learn the consonants and spell the Pinyin syllables on the building blocks.

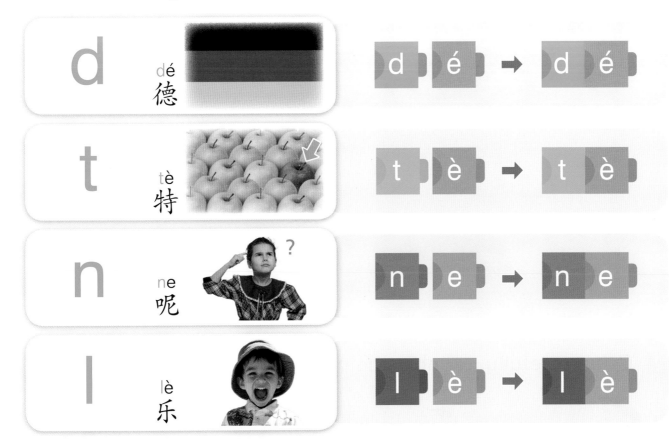

d	dé 德	d é → d é
t	tè 特	t è → t è
n	ne 呢	n e → n e
l	lè 乐	l è → l è

2 Listen carefully. Circle the correct Pinyin syllables.

1	dè	tè	nè	lè
2	dà	tà	nà	là
3	dí	tí	ní	lí
4	dǔ	tǔ	nǔ	lǔ
5	mǔ	fǔ	nǔ	lǔ

Consonants 声母 (3)

1 Learn the consonants and spell the Pinyin syllables on the building blocks.

2 Listen carefully. Number the penguins.

Consonants 声母 (4)

 1 Learn the consonants and spell the Pinyin syllables on the building blocks.

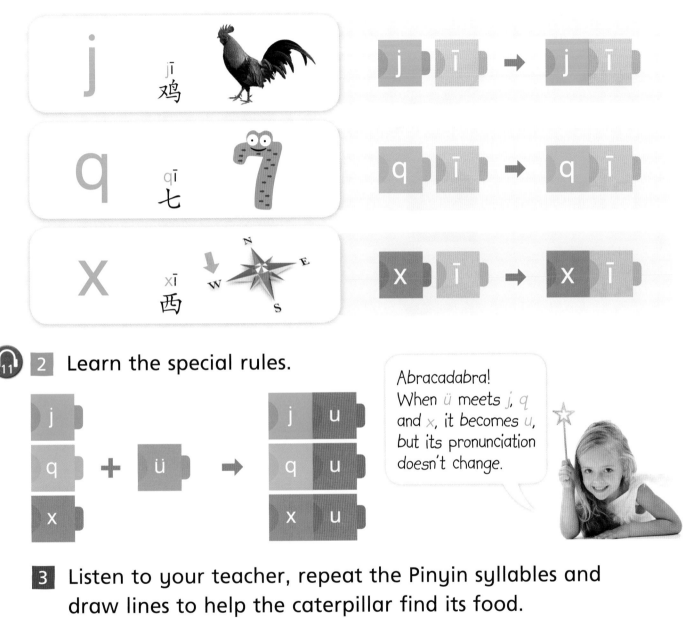

2 Learn the special rules.

> Abracadabra! When *ü* meets *j, q* and *x*, it becomes *u*, but its pronunciation doesn't change.

3 Listen to your teacher, repeat the Pinyin syllables and draw lines to help the caterpillar find its food.

jī	jí	jǐ	jì	jū	jú	jǔ	jù
qī	qí	qǐ	qì	qū	qú	qǔ	qù
xī	xí	xǐ	xì	xū	xú	xǔ	xù

Consonants 声母 (5)

12 **1** Learn the consonants and read the Pinyin syllables on the building blocks.

These four syllables are whole syllables. They are not spelt with separate consonants and vowels.

zh — zhī 枝 — zhī

ch — chī 吃 — chī

sh — shī 狮 — shī

r — rì 日 — rì

13 **2** Listen carefully. Circle the correct Pinyin syllables.

1	zhā	chā	shā	hā
2	zhè	chè	shè	rè
3	zhì	chì	shì	rì
4	zhǔ	chǔ	shǔ	rǔ

Consonants 声母 (6)

🎧 **1** Learn the consonants and read the Pinyin syllables on the building blocks.

💡 These three syllables are also whole syllables.

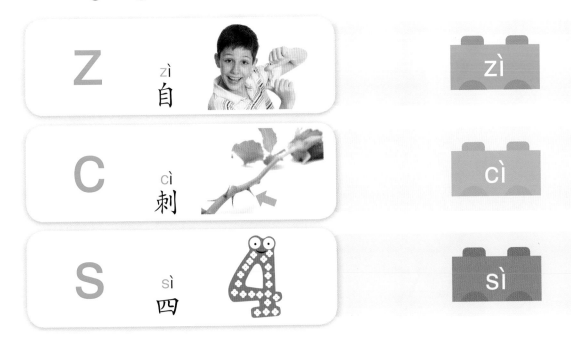

Z zì 自

C cì 刺

S sì 四

zì

cì

sì

🎧 **2** Listen carefully. Circle the correct carriages.

1 | zī | zhī | cī | chī | sī | shī

2 | zè | cè | zhè | chè | zhè | cè

3 | sù | chú | cù | shú | sù | zhú

Compound vowels 复韵母 (1)

16 **1** Learn the compound vowels and read them in the different tones.

> Some compound vowels are formed by combining single vowels.

ai　ǎi　矮　　　　 āi　ái　ǎi　ài

ei　ēi　欸　　　　ēi　éi　ěi　èi

ui　wèi　喂　　　　uī　uí　uǐ　uì

> The vowel *ui* has the same sound as the syllable *wei*.

2 Play with your friend. Read the Pinyin syllables on your path as you move forward.

duì　tāi　nèi

fēi　　　　　lěi

mǎi　　　　　　gěi

cuī　sāi

pèi　zuì　　　**Finish**　guī

zéi

bái　　　　　　　　kài

zǎi　　　　　huī

Start　ruì　shuǐ　zhái

Compound vowels 复韵母 (2)

1 Learn the compound vowels and read them in the different tones.

ao āo 凹 — āo áo ǎo ào

ou ōu 鸥 — ōu óu ǒu òu

iu yōu 优 — iū iú iǔ iù

💡 The vowel *iu* has the same sound as the syllable *you*.

2 Circle the Pinyin syllables with *ao*, *ou* and *iu*. Read them aloud.

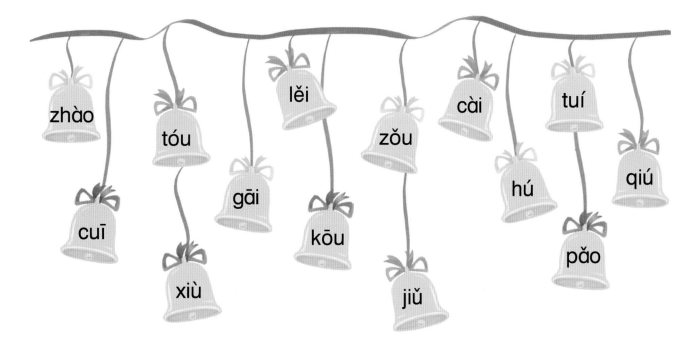

zhào
cuī
tóu
gāi
xiù
lěi
kōu
zǒu
jiǔ
cài
hú
pǎo
tuí
qiú

Compound vowels 复韵母 (3)

1 Learn the compound vowels and read them in the different tones.

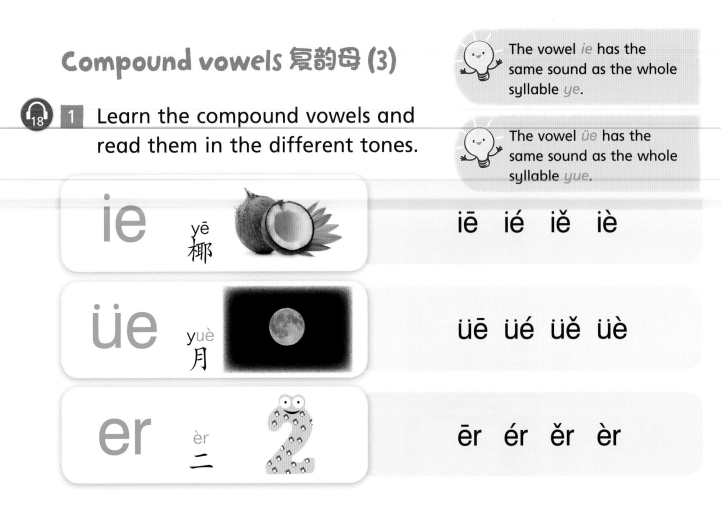

The vowel *ie* has the same sound as the whole syllable *ye*.

The vowel *üe* has the same sound as the whole syllable *yue*.

ie yē 椰	iē ié iě iè
üe yuè 月	üē üé üě üè
er èr 二	ēr ér ěr èr

2 Listen, repeat the Pinyin syllables and colour the puzzle pieces blue.

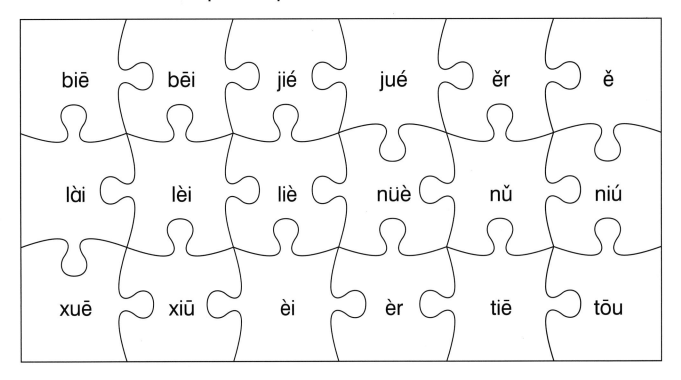

biē	bēi	jié	jué	ěr	ě
lài	lèi	liè	nüè	nǔ	niú
xuē	xiū	èi	èr	tiē	tōu

Compound vowels 复韵母 (4)

1 Learn the compound vowels and read them in the different tones.

an àn 岸

ān án ǎn àn

en èn 摁

ēn én ěn èn

in yīn 音

īn ín ǐn ìn

The vowel *in* has the same sound as the whole syllable *yin*.

2 Which Pinyin syllables have the vowels on the animals? Draw lines to link them and help the animals find their friends. Read the Pinyin syllables on the paths.

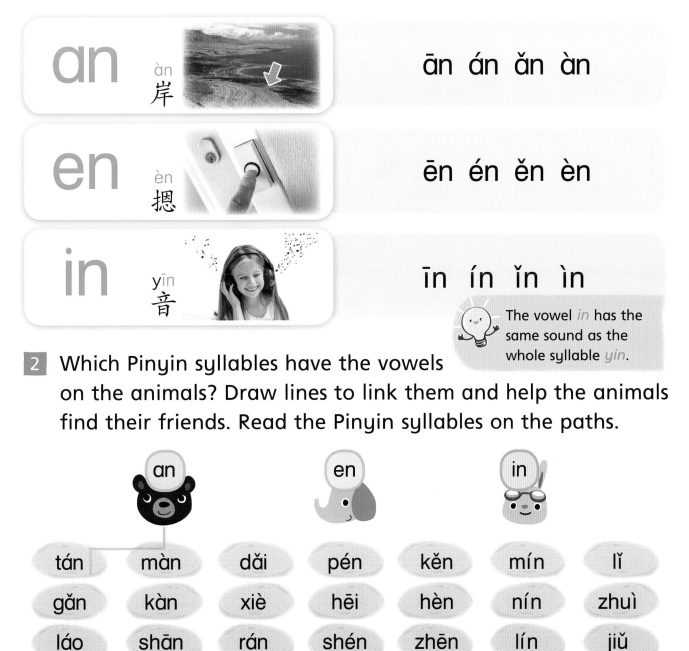

an   en   in

tán	màn	dǎi	pén	kěn	mín	lǐ
gǎn	kàn	xiè	hēi	hèn	nín	zhuì
láo	shān	rán	shén	zhēn	lín	jiǔ
chā	mài	càn	zěn	xīn	jìn	qiě

Compound vowels 复韵母 (5)

 Learn the compound vowels and read them in the different tones.

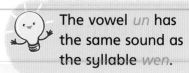
The vowel *un* has the same sound as the syllable *wen*.

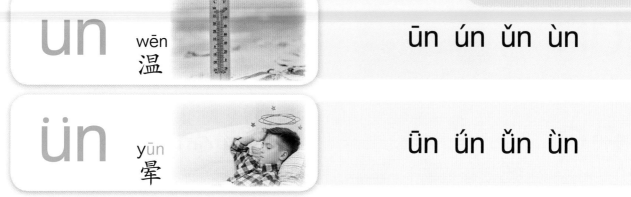

un   wēn 温   ūn   ún   ǔn   ùn

ün   yūn 晕   ūn   ún   ǔn   ùn

 2 Listen, repeat the Pinyin syllables and colour the shapes. Then count and write the numbers.

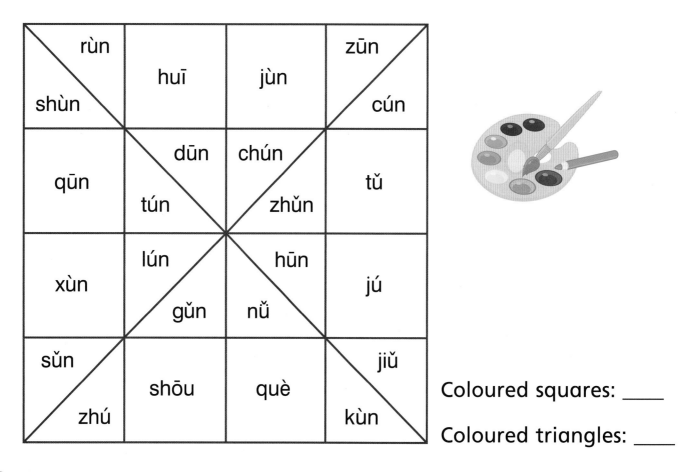

Coloured squares: ____

Coloured triangles: ____

(Syllables in grid: rùn, shùn, huī, jùn, zūn, cún, qūn, dūn, tún, chún, zhǔn, tǔ, xùn, lún, gǔn, hūn, nǔ, jú, sǔn, zhú, shōu, què, kùn, jiǔ)

16

Compound vowels 复韵母 (6)

1 Learn the compound vowels and read them in the different tones.

 The vowel *ing* has the same sound as the whole syllable *yǐng*.

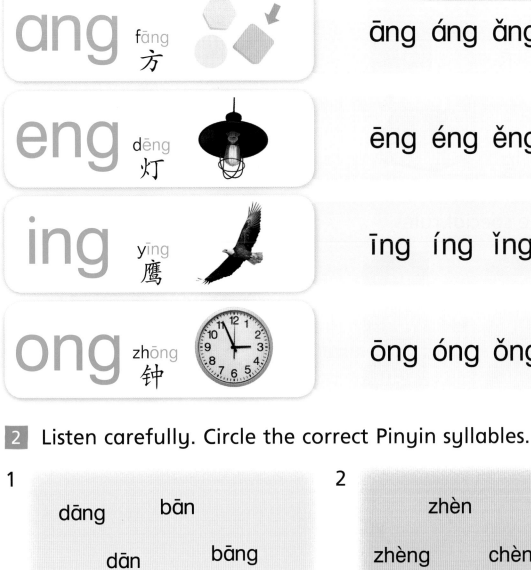

ang　fāng
方

āng　áng　ǎng　àng

eng　dēng
灯

ēng　éng　ěng　èng

ing　yīng
鹰

īng　íng　ǐng　ìng

ong　zhōng
钟

ōng　óng　ǒng　òng

2 Listen carefully. Circle the correct Pinyin syllables.

1

dāng　　bān

dān　　　bāng

2

zhèn　　　shèn

zhèng　　chèng

3

jīn　　　qìn

jìng　　qīng

4

dǒng

tǒng　　děng　　tǎng

Consonants 声母 (7)

25 **1** Learn the consonants and read the Pinyin syllables on the building blocks.

These two syllables are whole syllables.

y yī 衣

yī

w wū 屋

wū

26 **2** Learn the special rules.

y + ü → yu

üe → yue

ün → yun

When *ü* meets *y*, it becomes *u*, but its pronunciation doesn't change.

27 **3** Listen, repeat and join the Pinyin syllables to complete the animal.

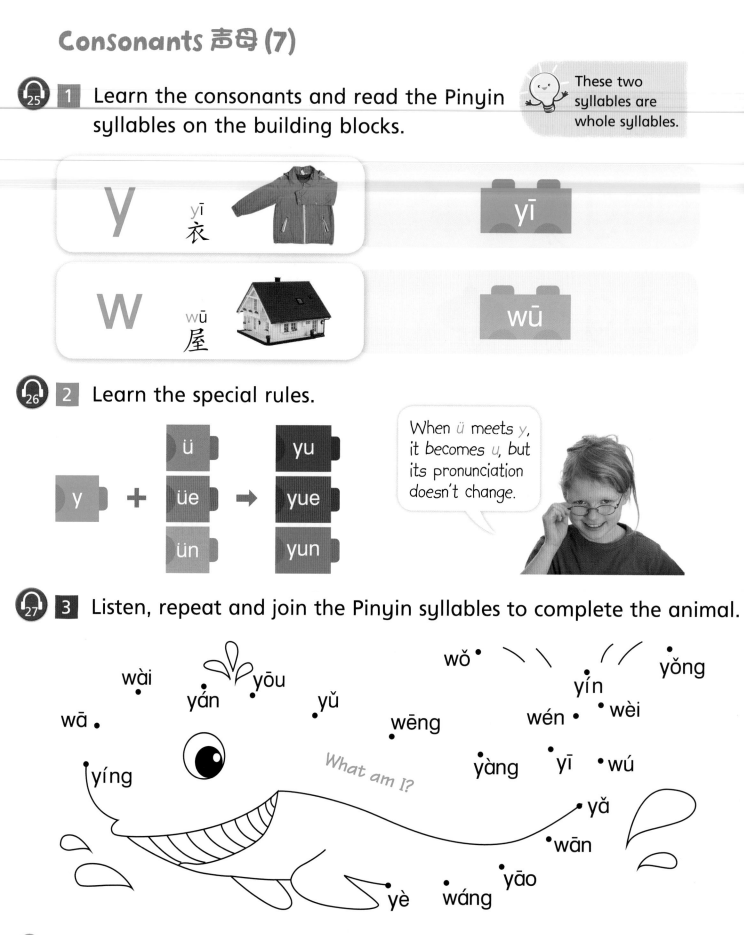

wài
yōu
wǒ
yǒng
yán
yǔ
yín
wēn
wèi
wā
wēng
yíng
yàng yī wú
What am I?
yǎ
wān
yāo
yè wáng

Pronunciation rules 拼读规则

 1 Some Pinyin syllables are made up of a consonant and a vowel. Look, listen and repeat.

Consonant + Vowel → Syllable

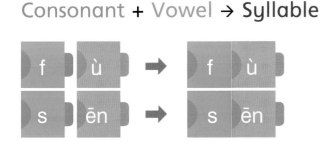

> We've already learnt this combination. Remember to pronounce the consonant quickly and lightly, and also stress the vowel.

2 Some Pinyin syllables have a single vowel *i*, *u* or *ü* as a middle vowel between the consonant and the final vowel. Look, listen and repeat.

Consonant + Middle vowel + Final vowel → Syllable

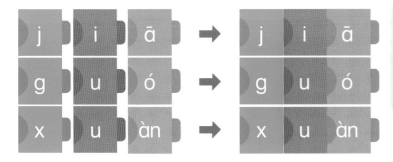

> Pronounce the consonant lightly and the middle vowel quickly, and stress the final vowel. Say the whole syllable without pauses in between.

3 Listen carefully. Circle the correct Pinyin syllables. Then repeat all the Pinyin syllables after your teacher.

1	láo	liáo	lán	lián
2	huā	huāi	huān	huāng
3	shà	shuài	shàn	shuò
4	mǎo	miǎo	mǎn	miǎn
5	xiā	xiāo	xiān	xiōng
6	jiǎn	jiǎng	juǎn	jiǒng

Whole syllables 整体认读音节

🎧 **30** Listen and repeat the 16 whole syllables. Remember that they are not spelt with separate consonants and vowels.

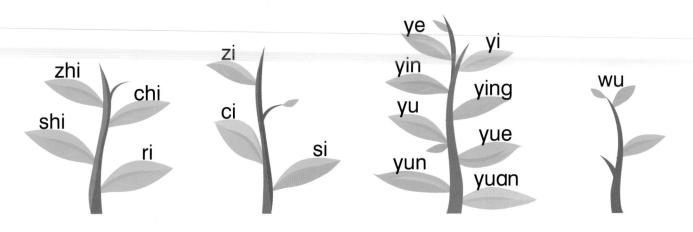

zhi chi shi ri
zi ci si
ye yi yin ying yu yue yun yuan
wu

Position of the tone marks 声调位置

🎧 **31** Learn the position of the tone marks. Say the chant and look at the Pinyin syllables.

a, o, e, i, u, ü,
Tone marks sit on these six letters.
i, u, ü, a, o, e,
First look for vowel *a.*
When vowel *a* is not there,
You should go for *o* or *e.*
If vowel *i* meets *u,*
The last letter takes the mark.

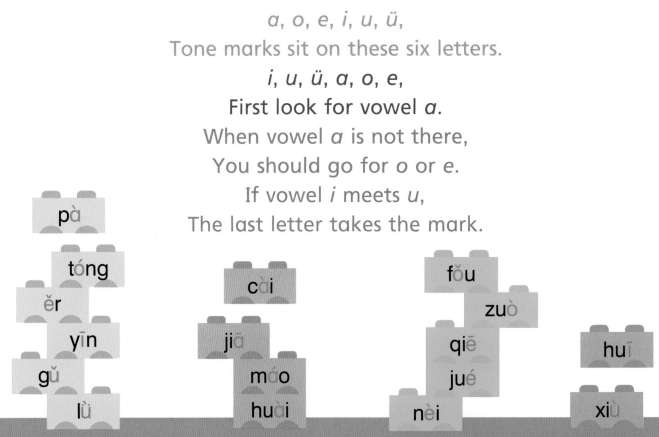

pà
tóng
ěr
yīn
gǔ
lù

cài
jiā
máo
huài

fǒu
zuò
qiē
jué
nèi

huī
xiù

The 'r' sound 儿化音

32 Learn the 'r' sound and repeat after the recording.

huā   huār

花 → 花儿

Sometimes, we add the suffix 儿 to a word in spoken Chinese. This changes the sound of the word.

In *huār*, the vowel *uā* combines with *r* to form a new sound.

zǐ
↓
zǐr

niǎo
↓
niǎor

wō
↓
wōr

Syllable-dividing mark(') 隔音符号

33 Some Pinyin syllables have the same letter combination, but they sound differently. How can we tell them apart? Learn the syllable-dividing mark and repeat after the recording.

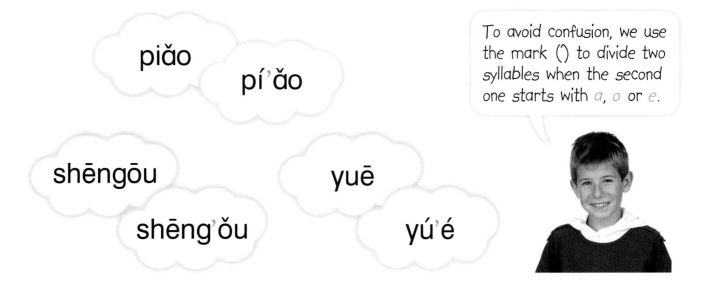

piǎo

pí'ǎo

To avoid confusion, we use the mark (') to divide two syllables when the second one starts with *a, o* or *e*.

shēngōu

yuē

shēng'ǒu

yú'é

Tone changes 变调

 In some cases, the tone of a character will change to a different one in spoken Chinese, although it is not shown in standard Pinyin. Learn the rules for tone changes.

1   Rules for 一 (one)
(yī)

yī + (–) → yì + (–)	yī tiān → yì tiān 一天 (one day)
yī + (ˊ) → yì + (ˊ)	yī zhí → yì zhí 一直 (always)
yī + (ˇ) → yì + (ˇ)	yī qǐ → yì qǐ 一起 (together)
yī + (ˋ) → yí + (ˋ)	yī bàn → yí bàn 一半 (half)

When 一 is followed by a character carrying the first, second or third tone, 一 changes to the fourth tone.

When 一 is followed by a character carrying the fourth tone, 一 changes to the second tone.

2   Rule for 不 (no)
(bù)

bù + (ˋ) → bú + (ˋ)	bù duì → bú duì 不对 (incorrect)

When 不 is followed by a character carrying the fourth tone, 不 changes to the second tone.

3   Rule for the third tone (ˇ)

(ˇ) + (ˇ) → (ˊ) + (ˇ)	xiǎo niǎo → xiáo niǎo 小鸟 (bird)

When two characters carrying the third tone are put together, the tone of the first character changes to the second tone.

Revision 复习

1 Read the Pinyin letters. Colour the boxes with consonants purple and the ones with vowels green.

a	o	i	ie	h	l	r	ong	j
f	üe	p	k	e	er	x	c	un

2 Read the Pinyin syllables and colour the decorations.

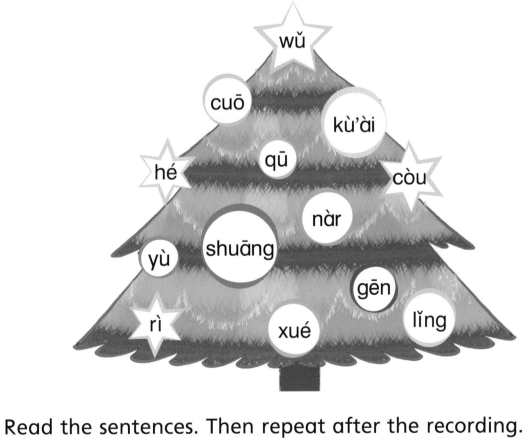

wǔ

cuō

kù'ài

qū

hé

còu

nàr

yù shuāng

gēn

rì xué lǐng

3 Read the sentences. Then repeat after the recording.

Jīn tiān xià le yī diǎnr yǔ
1 今天下了一点儿雨。

Xiǎo gǒu bù jiàn le   Tā qù nǎr le
2 小狗不见了。它去哪儿了？

Wǒ yǒu yī gè jiě jie
3 我有一个姐姐。

OXFORD
UNIVERSITY PRESS

Oxford University Press is a department of the University of Oxford.
It furthers the University's objective of excellence in research, scholarship,
and education by publishing worldwide. Oxford is a registered trade mark of
Oxford University Press in the UK and in certain other countries

Published in Hong Kong by
Oxford University Press (China) Limited
39th Floor, One Kowloon, 1 Wang Yuen Street, Kowloon Bay,
Hong Kong

Photographs for reproduction permitted by Dreamstime.com

China National Publications Import & Export (Group) Corporation is an authorized distributor of
Oxford Elementary Chinese.

Please contact content@cnpiec.com.cn or 86-10-65856782

ISBN: 978-0-19-082363-4

10 9 8 7 6 5 4 3